SCIENCE GETS PHYSICAL

Physical Science in FOOTBALL

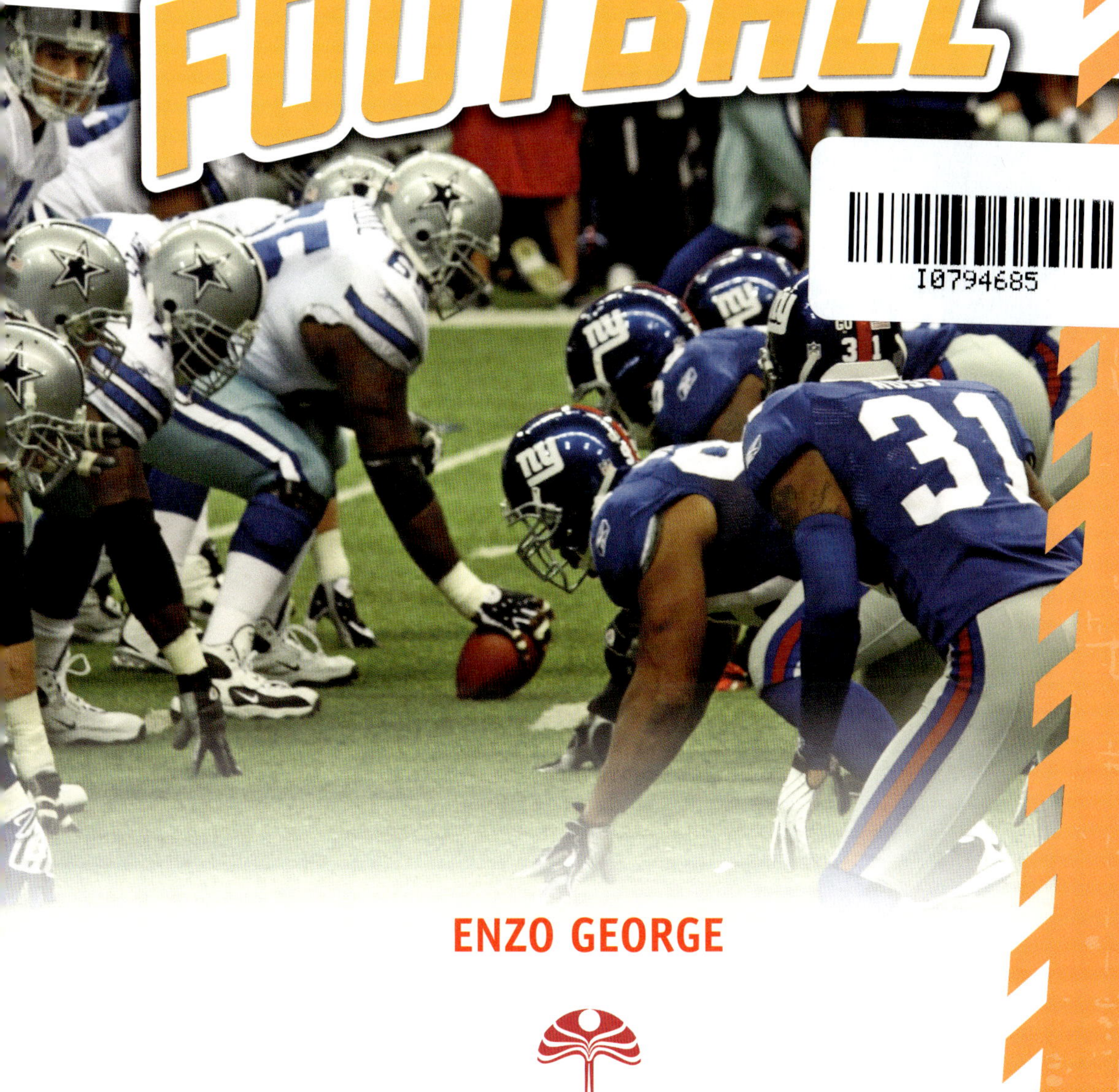

ENZO GEORGE

CRABTREE
PUBLISHING COMPANY
WWW.CRABTREEBOOKS.COM

Author: Enzo George
Editors: Sarah Eason, Jennifer Sanderson, and Elizabeth DiEmanuele
Consultant: David Hawksett
Editorial director: Kathy Middleton
Proofreader: Wendy Scavuzzo
Design: Paul Myerscough and Jeni Child
Design edits: Katherine Berti
Cover design: Lorraine Inglis
Photo research: Rachel Blount
Print and production coordinator: Katherine Berti

Written, developed, and produced by Calcium

Photo Credits:
t=Top, c=Center, b=Bottom, l= Left, r=Right

Inside: Inside: Shutterstock: Antpkr: p. 16; Aspen Photo: p. 3, 7t, 14, 25, 30, 32, 36, 38; Darios: p. 44; Ken Durden: p. 1, 41; Vincent Giordano Photo: p. 10; JoeSAPhotos: p. 9b, 12–13, 13b; Richard Paul Kane: p. 6–7, 24; Margaret Kite: p. 35; Herbert Kratky: p. 15, 26, 29, 31; Alexey Stiop: p. 23, 33; Sergey Mironov: p. 8–9t; Monkey Business Images: p. 4–5b; Amy Myers: p. 20; Sergey Nivens: p. 42–43t; Andrey_Popov: p. 19; Tracy Proffitt: p. 5t; Denys Prykhodov: p. 40; Rocketclips, Inc: p. 34; Alesanko Rodriguez: p. 37; Jerry Sharp: p. 17; Sirtravelalot: p. 39, 45; Mark Skalny: p. 18; Todd Taulman Photography: p. 21; Wikimedia Commons: Keith Allison: p. 11; Asilva of Flickr: p. 27; Department of Defense photo by U.S. Air Force Tech. Sgt. Michael R. Holzwort: p. 22; Fireblade9977: p. 40 (inset); Ozzy Trevino of U.S. Customs and Border Protection: p. 43b; User:B: p. 28

Cover: Shutterstock: Eugene Onischenko

Library and Archives Canada Cataloguing in Publication

Title: Physical science in football / Enzo George.
Names: George, Enzo, author.
Description: Series statement: Science gets physical | Includes index.
Identifiers: Canadiana (print) 20190195436 | Canadiana (ebook) 20190195444 | ISBN 9780778775461 (hardcover) | ISBN 9780778776352 (softcover) | ISBN 9781427125217 (HTML)
Subjects: LCSH: Football—Juvenile literature.
Classification: LCC GV950.7 .G46 2020 | DDC j796.332—dc23

Library of Congress Cataloging-in-Publication Data

CIP available at the Library of Congress

LCCN: 2019043958

Crabtree Publishing Company
www.crabtreebooks.com 1-800-387-7650

Printed in the U.S.A./012020/CG20191115

Published in Canada
Crabtree Publishing
616 Welland Ave.
St. Catharines, Ontario
L2M 5V6

Published in the United States
Crabtree Publishing
PMB 59051
350 Fifth Avenue, 59th Floor
New York, New York 10118

Published in the United Kingdom
Crabtree Publishing
Maritime House
Basin Road North, Hove
BN41 1WR

Published in Australia
Crabtree Publishing
Unit 3 - 5 Currumbin Court
Capalaba
QLD 4157

CONTENTS

CHAPTER 1

SCIENCE ON THE FIELD

Football is the most popular game in the United States. It brings in thousands of players and millions of fans. Fans come to watch coaches try to outsmart each other. Some have called football a game of chess on a playing field.

Understanding the physics of football might not help you catch a pass. But it might explain why you dropped it!

Quarterbacks throw at least 30 passes in a game. Every pass obeys the same laws of motion.

Sport for All

Football has something for everyone. It can be very thoughtful, because teams use tactics to gain an advantage. It can also be violent, as powerful players smash each other to the ground. Players can be any size or shape. They range from huge linemen to tall, slim receivers. They can also be smaller, more athletic running backs.

It might not seem like it with so many crashes and collisions, but football is also all about **physics**. For example, why does the ball travel farther if it travels point-first? The answer to this question is all about **air resistance** and **friction**, or drag. There are other parts of the game that involve physics. The reason a tackler aims for a runner's legs is because of **torque**. Torque is a turning **force.** It means a low hit will cause the runner's body to swing forward. Players wear helmets to protect their heads because of **kinetic energy** and **impact**.

Super Computer!

Most football players may not know about the laws of physics. They play the way they do for many reasons. Maybe a play seems natural, or their coaches have told them to do it. But, without knowing it, players are figuring out math and physics problems all the time. The brain of the quarterback is one of the most advanced math computers on Earth! They can make a play while 21 other players are moving.

Running and Throwing

The aim of football is to score points. Players need to get the ball into the end zone at either end of the field. There are many different ways to achieve this. Teams have playbooks that describe the precise movements of individual players. They do this for hundreds of different plays. Those plays can be complicated. They are designed to try to create holes in the defensive line for a running back, or to make space up the field, so a receiver is open to catch a pass or stop an attack. There are so many possible calls for any play. Coaches on the sidelines often use tablets to figure out the best choice. They then communicate it to the quarterback from a radio linked to speakers inside the helmet.

This quarterback pulls their right arm back to get as great a forward movement as possible to transfer energy to the ball.

Moving the Ball Forward

It sometimes seems as though there are endless possible plays, but there are only three ways to move the ball forward. A player can carry it, throw it, or punt it. Carrying the ball forward involves a runner being able to speed up quickly. Running backs are good at **acceleration**. This gives them an advantage over a short distance. They can reach full **velocity** faster than defenders.

Throwing and Punting

The second way of getting the ball forward is for someone to throw it. This is usually the quarterback, who is a specialist thrower. A team can make one forward pass in a play. The team uses passes to go over or around the many players in the middle of the field. A ball travels through the air faster than a player can travel across the ground. This is because the ball is lighter and is **streamlined**, so it is not slowed down much by air resistance. Players are heavier than the ball and are more affected by air resistance. They also gain more friction when their feet hit the ground. The friction slows them down more.

Punting the ball involves kicking it in a high **arc** into the air. This kick almost always results in the opposition gaining possession of the ball, so teams use it as a way to gain as much area as they can. That way, the opposition starts its attack as far back as possible.

By swinging their foot from one side to the other, kickers try to make the ball ***spiral*** *as it flies.*

GETTING PHYSICAL: LAWS OF MOTION

Many moves in football show Newton's Laws of Motion. These laws are from the 1680s. They were explained by the English scientist Sir Isaac Newton. The First Law states that an object will remain at rest or moving at the same speed in a straight line. The object will move unless it is compelled to change its state by an external force. This "sameness" is known as **inertia**. The Second Law explains how the velocity of an object changes when it is subjected to an external force. The force creates a proportional change in **momentum**, which is equal to **mass** x velocity. The Third Law states that for every action (or force), there is an equal and opposite reaction.

Anatomy of a Football Player

A football team succeeds or fails together. But within the team, every individual has specific tasks. The defensive linemen use their strength to protect the quarterback. The offensive linemen try to push their way past them. These forwards are usually large and heavy. So, they are difficult to shove out of the way. They have a low **center of mass**, so they are hard to push over. They have strong legs to propel them into impacts with the player facing them. They also have powerful upper bodies and arms with which to grapple.

*Players at the **line of scrimmage** crouch down to lower their centers of mass.*

Running Backs

Behind the offensive line, running backs are ready to carry the ball into the line of forwards. They try to find a way through any gaps the linemen are able to open up. Running backs tend to be small but powerful. They have fantastic balance, and they can cut, or change direction very quickly to trick tacklers. This move puts great pressure on their joints, especially on their knees. Many knee injuries occur when the knee twists sideways during a run. Running backs' speed is usually measured in the time it takes for them to run the 40-yard (37 m) dash.

Speed Kings

Wide receivers often have to run farther. They are the real sprinters on the team, together with the safeties, who have to try to stop them. Receivers have more room in front of them before they come into contact with defenders, so they can accelerate more slowly than running backs. They accelerate slowly, even though their greatest velocity is usually higher.

GETTING PHYSICAL: ACCELERATION

In physics, the idea of acceleration applies not only to an object speeding up, but also to any change in velocity or direction. For some positions, the rate at which players accelerate is most important. It can be even more important than their highest velocity. For example, running backs have to be able to speed up, brake suddenly, and cut to avoid blockers.

They are often tall and lightweight, so they have a long stride for running and can launch themselves to grab a pass from high in the air. The safeties are equally as fast. They must constantly change direction to try to cover a pass. If a receiver catches the ball, it is a race. The safety must figure out the route that gives him the best chance of catching up to the player with the ball.

The quarterback is an all-round athlete. They control the offensive plays. They either hand off the ball to a running back, or throw it forward. At any time, the quarterback has to calculate the likely chances of success for any option. They can vary the play at any time, too.

Players do not always have to be super-fast. It is possible to beat defenders using agility rather than pure speed.

CHAPTER 2

HAVING A BALL

The white lines at the ends of the football are guides that help players. Using the lines, they can see how it is spinning in the air.

At the heart of football is the ball that gives the game its name. It might seem strange that a sport where the ball is mostly thrown and caught with the hands is called football. Before the 1870s, the ball could only be kicked.

The Ball

The ball looks like a sphere that has been flattened in the middle. It has points on both ends. Together, this creates a shape called a prolate spheroid. This shape makes the ball bounce in an unpredictable way. A regular sphere bounces off a flat surface at exactly the opposite angle, in the same direction. But, the shape of the football changes this. The football can bounce off the ground in almost any direction. The direction depends on exactly which part of it hits the ground. This is why football players try to catch the ball without letting it bounce.

The unusual shape of the ball came from the animal **bladders** that were originally used to play the game. They were not a regular shape. The first leather footballs were shaped a little like melons. The football gradually changed into the modern design.

Making the Ball

Balls are made from four panels of leather. These panels are lined with a **synthetic** material to keep them from stretching out of shape. The panels are stitched together on the long sides, leaving one seam open. An airtight rubber bladder is pushed in through the open seam. The bladder is the same shape as the ball, but it is a little smaller. The open seam is then closed with white laces, which help players grip the ball. The leather is stamped to create an uneven surface called pebbling. Pebbling increases the surface area of the ball. An increased surface area means that more of the ball comes into contact with players' hands. More contact increases friction, which gives players a better grip on the leather.

SCIENCE WINS!

ALL ABOUT THE AIR

Footballs are inflated with air. The air pressure affects how the ball handles. In January 2015, an American Football Conference (AFC) playoff game was played between the New England Patriots and the Indianapolis Colts. The Patriots quarterback Tom Brady (photo below) was accused of ordering air to be let out of balls. A softer ball is easier to grip because the surface molds to the players' hands, creating more pressure. Brady denied the charge, but he was suspended for four games as a punishment.

Flight of the Ball

The scores are tight with seconds to go. The offense has the ball in its own half of the field. The **snap** is taken. The quarterback waits before launching a **Hail Mary** pass. The ball arcs high into the air. It reaches the top of its flight, then it falls back smoothly toward the ground—straight into the arms of a receiver sprinting for the touchdown.

The receiver must be in the right place to catch the ball as gravity pulls it back to the ground.

Go Long!

A long pass is one of the most spectacular sights in football. But, throwing the ball such long distances makes it difficult to control. Teams usually attempt Hail Mary passes only toward the end of the game when they fear they will lose the game by more than they need to.

Long passes and kicks travel a path through the air called a **parabola**, or arc. The ball has projectile motion, which means it is affected by the force of **gravity** as it travels. The ball has both horizontal motion and vertical motion. Horizontal motion carries the ball down the field. Vertical motion is determined by the angle at which the ball is thrown or kicked into the air. To get the greatest range, the ball needs to be launched at an angle of 45 degrees.

Air Resistance

Gravity is the major force acting on the path of the ball. The other force is air resistance, which is the drag created on the ball as it pushes its way through the **molecules**, or tiny particles, in the air. When the ball travels point-first in a pass, the shape of the ball makes air slip over the surface, so drag is very low. But, for a punt or field goal, the ball travels end over end. That increases air resistance. So, the arc of the ball has to carry it higher to travel the same distance.

GETTING PHYSICAL: THROWING A SPIRAL

When the quarterback throws a long pass, they use their fingers and wrist to make the ball spin. The ball spins around its own **axis**. This gives the ball angular momentum, which is a rotation that stays constant. This means the ball stays in the same orientation: its nose points down the field and slightly upward. This reduces air resistance and makes the ball's path more accurate.

Special Teams

The only time football really lives up to its name is when teams kick the ball. Kicking is a special skill. Teams have dedicated kickers who are part of the special teams. They come onto the field to take a kick-off or to kick field goals after touchdowns. They may also punt the ball away at the end of an **offensive drive**. They will do this if it is unlikely that a team will gain 10 yards (9 m) on a fourth **down**.

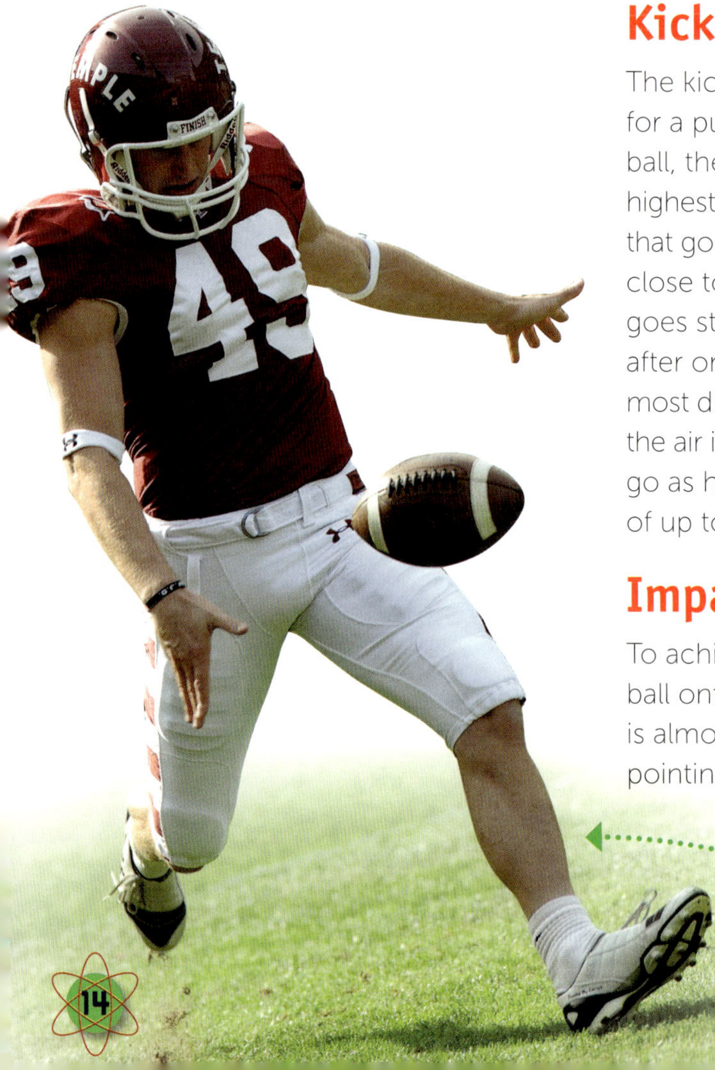

Kicking Skills

The kicker kicks the ball from their hands for a punt. To get most distance on the ball, the kicker needs to kick it at the highest speed and at the best angle. A punt that goes straight up in the air will land very close to where it was kicked. A punt that goes straight along the ground will land after only a short distance. To gain the most distance, the ball needs to go up into the air in a path called a parabola. It might go as high as 120 feet (37 m) at speeds of up to 90 miles per hour (145 kph).

Imparting Velocity

To achieve this, the kicker drops the ball onto their swinging foot. The ball is almost level, with the ball's nose pointing slightly upward.

The kicker draws their kicking leg as far back as possible to gain the greatest momentum to transfer energy to the ball.

A teammate holds the ball in a vertical position on the ground to allow the kicker to get their foot beneath it.

This position makes sure that as much of the ball comes into contact with the top of the foot as possible. The kick can then transmit the most force to the ball. Once it leaves the foot, the ball is affected by two types of velocity. Its horizontal velocity is how fast it travels across the ground. Its vertical velocity is how fast it rises into the air. As the ball reaches the top of the arc, there is a moment when it has no vertical velocity. This moment happens before the effect of gravity makes it begin falling back to Earth.

End-Over-End

A kick-off or field goal gets kicked from a tee or from the ground where it is supported by a player. The ball is nearly upright when it is kicked, so the kicker's foot catches the ball at its bottom end. This makes the ball rotate end-over-end through the air. It encounters air resistance each time it spins, which slows it down. That means the ball must be kicked with more energy than if it traveled end-on.

GETTING PHYSICAL: LEGS AS LEVERS

A **lever** is a tool that multiplies force. It is usually a long bar, or a similar shape, which rotates from a **fulcrum**. The fulcrum can be placed along the length of the lever. It is used to transfer an opposite force from one end of the lever to the other. It can also be placed at one end of the lever, which is the case with a kicker's leg. When a kicker kicks, their leg rotates around the fulcrum formed by their hip. To gain the most power, the lever must be as long as possible. So their leg should be straight when it makes contact with the ball. The foot is the point of greatest speed. If the kicker were to hit the ball closer toward the fulcrum, it would not generate the same amount of force.

CHAPTER 3

EQUIPMENT

You can play football nearly anywhere there is enough space to run and catch. The surface of the ground that you play on does not really matter. The ball rarely bounces. But, it would hurt to get tackled to the ground on concrete!

The Field

For an official game, the field is 160 feet (49 m) wide and 100 yards (91.4 m) long. There is a 10-yard (9.1 m) end zone at each end. The playing field is marked off with a solid line every 10 yards (9.1 m). There are also two parallel rows of 2-foot-long (0.6 m) hash lines in the center of the field, where the rows are 18.5 feet (5.6 m) apart. The hash lines mark every yard on the field and are used to place the ball for downs.

Precise measuring is important. The field is marked to help officials and players judge forward movement.

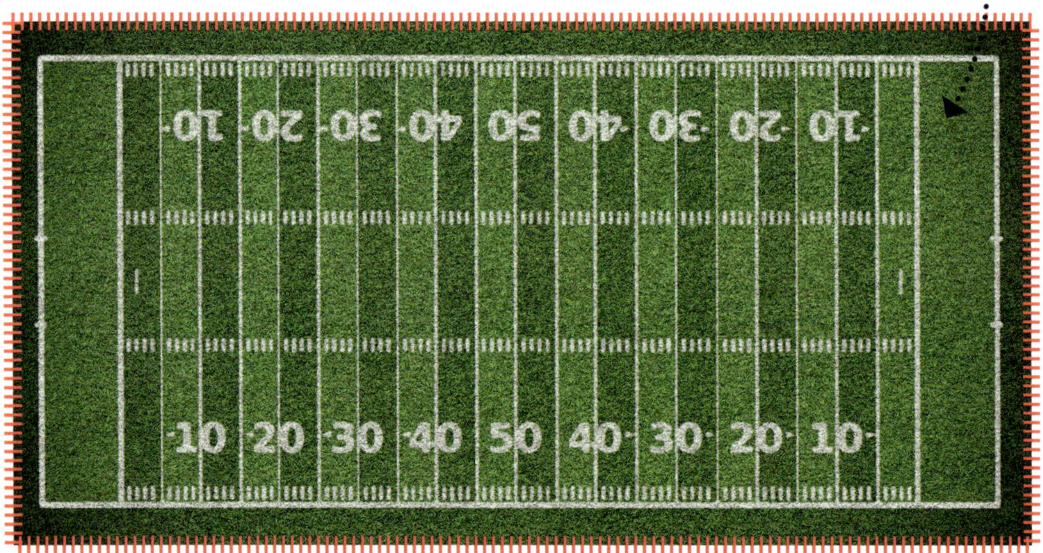

The goalposts are T-shaped so that players do not run into them. The crossbar is 10 feet (3 m) above the ground, and 18 feet 6 inches (5.6 m) wide. The two posts rise for 20 feet (6.1 m) above the crossbar.

About 12 National Football League (NFL) football fields have natural grass. The remaining 17 have astroturf, or artificial turf. This "grass" is made from synthetic fibers such as nylon. The fibers are woven into mats, often made of rubber, that fit closely together in the field.

The spaces between the tufts are usually filled with sand or pellets of rubber. Artificial turf has some advantages. It is stronger, and does not need sunlight, water, or mowing. It is especially useful in domes or stadiums, but some people complain that artificial turf increases injuries. Injuries can happen when players' **cleats** get caught and they twist their legs. They can also happen when the grass "burns" players' skin when they slide on it.

All-Weather Pitches

NFL games are never canceled because of the weather, even if it snows. For this reason, the fields with natural grass almost all have under-turf heating. In this system, a network of miles of thin pipes is laid beneath the surface. Frozen soil can be as hard as concrete, because droplets of water trapped in the soil freeze and become ice. In under-turf heating, hot water is pumped through the pipes, melting the frozen ground above.

Many players prefer to play on grass, because both the ball and the cleats grip grass well.

Helmet and Pads

No one wants to get hurt playing a sport, but football is a game with many collisions, so injuries are unavoidable. Engineers have come up with ways to make the game as safe as possible. Players wear helmets and body pads that protect their shoulders, hips, thighs, and knees.

Some players wear a line of eye black beneath their eyes. It helps avoid glare by cutting down on sunlight reflected into their eyes from their skin.

Helmets and Facemasks

The helmet is traditionally made from a hard shell of plastic. It has padding made from foam rubber or inflated with air. Inflatable pads keep the helmet molded to the player's head. Foam jaw pads keep the helmet fitted to their face. A chinstrap holds the helmet in place. The shell is designed to absorb force during an impact. The force of impact moves into the helmet, which crumples. This prevents the impact from going to the player's head.

Players choose facemasks that provide either greater protection or better visibility. Attached to the facemasks are mouthguards made from plastic. The plastic is softened in warm water, then the player bites into it, and it hardens to form a perfect fit for their mouth. The force of an impact can cause the lower jaw to snap into the upper one. The mouth guard prevents players biting their tongues or damaging their teeth.

Shoulder and body pads give football players their top-heavy appearance.

Hidden Voices

Since 1994, quarterback helmets have small speakers near the ears. The speakers allow coaches to call plays from the sideline, without a timeout. Originally, this communication came from radio signals. Today, it is from wireless Internet technology.

Advanced Protection

Most clashes between players happen with the shoulders, so shoulder pads are very important. They are made from padded foam covered by a hard shell of plastic. Small, overlapping shells cover the top of the arm and the shoulder joints. Hard body pads go over the shoulders and lace at the front of the body to protect the ribs. The design of the pads allows them to absorb some of the energy from an impact, then spreads that energy over a larger area.

SCIENCE WINS!

DICK'S NIGHT TRAIN

Dick Lane was one of the most feared tacklers in NFL history. In the 1950s and 1960s, he was a defensive back for many teams. Teams included the Chicago Cardinals and Detroit Lions. Lane was nicknamed "Night Train," because he often grabbed players around the neck and facemask. This move was legal at the time. He explained that, if he tackled someone by the legs, they might be able to fall down and gain ground. By tackling them around the neck, he could prevent that. Lane's tackling directly led to the NFL banning facemask tackles. It also led to a ban on neck tackles.

Gloves and Cleats

Shoes are often forgotten in football. But, if a player wears the wrong footwear, it will soon become difficult for them to play.

Get a Grip

There are many types of shoes made by many manufacturers, but they all have to provide grip. There are two main ways of achieving grip. Artificial turf can be slippery, so shoes should have rippled patterns or small points molded into the rubber soles. These ripples increase the surface area so more of the shoe is in contact with the ground. A greater surface area improves grip. On grass fields, players wear cleats or studs that sink into the soil, again improving the grip.

*This image shows how players use **studs** in their shoes to help push off on soft grass.*

GETTING PHYSICAL: CATCH IT!

Many receivers wear special gloves to help them catch the ball. These gloves have palms made of rubber. Some have a sticky substance, such as **rosin** on them. This substance is viscoelastic, which means it has the qualities of both a solid and a liquid. It "flows" into tiny gaps on the surface of the glove. This increases the surface area of the glove, and the friction between the ball and glove.

Cleats and Studs

There are different sorts of cleats for different positions and different conditions. The studs can be different lengths and shapes depending on how damp and soft the ground is. Rigid studs help receivers speed up fast. Flexible material is better for players, such as running backs, who need to twist and turn. Some manufacturers use bladed studs to help acceleration, and cone-shaped studs for a wide range of movement. A chevron shape, which is a kind of V-shape, allows fast acceleration, quick changes of direction, and sudden braking.

Modern studs tend to be as small in diameter as possible. Research suggests that small studs dig into the ground better. They also release from the ground faster, so players do not get "stuck." There have also been other improvements, such as coating cleats with a film of plastic to keep out water and mud. This prevents the shoes from becoming clogged up.

Placing the Studs

Shoe design is complex. Engineers use digital analysis on computers to design the position of studs on the bottom of the shoe. They use a player's weight and foot size to figure out where the most pressure will be on the shoe. They then place the studs in the best positions so they all bear the same amounts of pressure.

CHAPTER 4

THE QUARTERBACK

On many NFL teams, the quarterback is the star and the most valuable player (MVP), but no quarterback can win on their own. Even legends need support from their forwards and backs. You cannot pass the ball anywhere if the other team has it or if you are lying on your back!

Throwing Power

Some quarterbacks can throw farther than others. Some can throw a tighter spiral, helping them be more accurate at longer distances. But, all good quarterbacks have a strong throwing arm. As they bring their arm forward and snap the elbow straight, the forearm, wrist, and hand act as a lever. Together, they send force from the shoulder and the muscles of the upper arm to the ball. This magnifies the force as it travels along the arm.

Peyton Manning threw 5,477 yards (5,008 m) for the Denver Broncos in 2013, a record for an NFL quarterback.

As the quarterback calls the play behind the scrimmage, they watch the opposition, in case they need to change their plans.

Big Hands

Quarterbacks often have large hands. Large hands help them to spread their fingers wide to get the best grip on the ball. Some have such large hands that they can keep hold of the ball even after they go through their throwing motion. If they see that a pass could be stopped, they hold on. To do this when their hand is traveling forward is hard. It requires keeping the pressure on the ball with the fingertips and the palm. This causes friction, which helps the ball "stick" to the hand.

Seeing Everything

The best quarterbacks can anticipate how the field will look in a few seconds' time. They have to be aware of their own receivers and the other team. Their brains have to process where a player will be and if they will be open by the time the ball reaches them. No one knows exactly how quarterbacks do this, but some researchers believe their brains have a special ability. They can figure out positioning on the field. Quarterbacks also need good peripheral vision. This is the ability to see out of the corners of their eyes. While they are searching for an open receiver, they need to know what is happening at the line of scrimmage. If a lineman gets through, the quarterback needs to take action.

Threading the Needle

Hitting a receiver with a hard, fast pass through a crowd of defenders is sometimes known as "threading the needle." The window through which the ball has to pass to avoid interceptions is sometimes tiny. The pass has to be close to perfect to succeed.

Nathan Scheelhaase of Illinois throws a pass off balance, after he has rolled out of the pocket during a play.

Velocity Vector

Whenever someone throws a football, it has both a direction and a length. The length depends on how hard the person throws the ball. In science, any quality with direction and length is called a vector. When the ball is released, it has a velocity vector. A velocity vector is usually shown on a diagram as an arrow. The length of the arrow indicates the length of the pass. For a good quarterback, the speed is about 45 to 50 miles per hour (72 to 80 kph). But, in a football game, there is usually more than one velocity vector. Unless the quarterback is standing behind a very good line, they are often in motion. When the player moves out of the **pocket**, they have their own velocity vector. Whatever direction they run in, they will have to throw in a different direction to get the ball to where the receiver will be when it arrives.

The receiver also has their own velocity vector. These factors mean that the quarterback will have to throw the ball at a different speed and path. The quarterback may throw the ball in a high arc to try to pass it over any oncoming defenders, or hard and flat, so it thuds into the receiver's **midriff**. A flat pass has far less distance to travel than an arced pass, so it reaches the receiver faster. This may allow the thrower to be more accurate, too.

The hardest part? The quarterback has to figure all this out in a few seconds!

GETTING PHYSICAL: PARALLELOGRAM VECTOR

It is possible to use math to figure out the velocity vector of a pass. To do this, you need to add together the vector of the pass and the vector of the moving quarterback. These vectors are two lines that represent two joining sides of a parallelogram. A parallelogram is a four-sided shape. It has two matching pairs of opposite parallel lines. By completing the missing sides, you can figure out the velocity vector at which the ball needs to be thrown. It is the length of the diagonal line of the parallelogram. Of course, no one draws a parallelogram on a football field, but this is a perfect way for mathematicians to use geometry in real life.

While the quarterback's forwards protect them from the opposing defenders, they look for a pass upfield.

Kinematics

Quarterbacks have strong arms. To throw a football more than 50 yards (46 m) takes a lot of power, but it is not just power that determines how far a pass can travel. The angle at which the quarterback launches the ball is also important.

Kinematics in Practice

The study of motion in terms of time and distance is called **kinematics**. The study does not think about the source of energy, but instead focuses on its path. Kinematics tries to find out an object's position, velocity, and acceleration at any stage in the object's path. In physics, acceleration includes any situation in which the object's speed or direction changes.

A quarterback throws a pass. As they do, they look downfield at their receivers, not at the ball.

A quarterback takes the easiest route past defenders by throwing the ball over their heads.

Kinematics uses math to describe the basic geometry of the system. In the case of a long football pass, the basic geometry is a parabola. Math is also used to analyze the starting points of the pass. Starting points include the position of the quarterback, weight of the ball, the ball's angle and velocity when it begins in flight, and its acceleration when it leaves the quarterback's hand. Using this information, mathematicians can figure out the path of the ball. They can figure out how high it will go. They can also figure out how fast it will travel.

Newton's Second Law of Motion says that the force on an object is equal to its mass multiplied by its acceleration. When the quarterback throws the ball, it accelerates from a still position, then travels through the air. If the football is heavier, the quarterback has to throw it with more force to get the same acceleration.

SCIENCE WINS!

MIRACLE AT MICHIGAN

In 1994, the Colorado Buffaloes were trailing the Michigan Wolverines 26–21. They had six seconds left. From near the 30-yard (27 m) line, Colorado quarterback Kordell Stewart threw a Hail Mary pass 70 yards (64 m) into the Michigan end zone. It was caught for a touchdown. That required Stewart to apply a lot of force to the ball, which is measured as work. In physics, work is done when a force is applied to an object over a distance. Stewart's effort was huge, but it was worth it. Colorado won the game 27–26. His pass is known as the "Miracle at Michigan."

CHAPTER 5

RUNNING AND TACKLING

Most football players never pass the ball. Some do not even touch the ball! But everyone has to be able to run and almost everyone has to tackle at one time or another. That means they are subject to a whole set of forces. These forces explain how they run and change direction. They also explain what happens when they collide with a player on the other team.

Momentum

Players of different sizes can reach the same momentum. Some just speed up at a different rate. Momentum is gained from multiplying mass by velocity. A smaller-but-fast runner has the same momentum as a heavier-but-slower forward. In football, this is important for defenders who are tackling or blocking attackers, and for trying to break through tackles.

Players at the line of scrimmage are separated by a neutral zone that is as wide as the length of the ball.

The amount of force needed to stop a runner is the same as the amount of force they can create while running. This depends on the runner's mass and acceleration. A runner of about 220 pounds (100 kg) accelerates quickly by pushing with their feet against the ground. According to Newton's Third Law of Motion, for every action there is an equal and opposite reaction. If the runner pushes against the turf with a force of 500 pounds (227 kg), the turf pushes back with equal force. This force allows them to generate speed. Once the runner is up to speed, they need a force of about 500 pounds (227 kg) to stop them. This could come from a smaller player running faster, or a larger player moving slower.

Tackling Power

When players have momentum, tacklers stop them by applying **impulse** in the opposite direction. Impulse is a combination of force plus time. Grabbing hold of a player for a long time can produce as much impulse as a quick hit.

Getting hold of a player and not letting go is a way to generate impulse in a tackle.

On the Move

The ball is snapped. The line of scrimmage comes alive as ten linemen clash and block each other. There seems to be no way through the wall of players. Then the quarterback hands off the ball to a running back. The running back twists and turns their way through. They use their speed, strength, and balance to pick out a path that only they can see.

A running back uses a sudden change of speed or direction to get past the dive of a defender.

Running Backs

The motion of a running back is an illustration of the concepts of kinematics. For a running back, the ability to accelerate rapidly is a great advantage. This is because there is little space to gain speed before they reach the line. By the time the running back reaches the forwards trying to block them, they are traveling fast. They need to be traveling so fast that they do not have time to react to their movements.

GETTING PHYSICAL: BALANCE

Balance is important for a running back. They have to be able to change direction and bounce off blocks and tackles without falling over. Balance is controlled by the **vestibular system** in the body. It depends on the movement of liquid in tiny organs in the inner ear. The movement of the liquid sends messages to the brain about how the body is oriented in space. Other messages come from the muscles and joints. Good balance also takes practice. Athletes, dancers, and others with outstanding balance practice hard to make their brains more effective at keeping them on their feet.

Changing Direction

A running back needs the ability to suddenly change direction. This puts pressure on their legs. While they run, they have inertia that will keep them going. They keep going in the same direction unless another force interferes. In this case, the runner's own legs halt their momentum. This happens as they change direction. The Third Law of Motion states that for every action there is an equal and opposite reaction. As the running back plants their foot to change direction, the force of their forward momentum pushes down on the ground. The ground pushes back with equal force. The foot and leg absorb the impact. This happens before the foot pushes off again in a different direction. Again, the ground pushes back with equal force. In the change of direction, the runner loses energy. So, the runner has to push off harder to maintain the same velocity.

The sudden changes of direction place great pressure on the knees, which are designed to absorb upward and downward pressure, but they are not designed for sideways pressure. A twist in the knee can damage important **ligaments**. Many running backs in the NFL suffer knee injuries, and some are bad enough to end the players' careers.

Tackle!

There are about 100 bone-crunching tackles that knock players to the ground. Sometimes, players get hit so hard that they drop the ball. Then, the tackler's team takes it. It is important to tackle as hard as possible because of Newton's Second Law of Motion. The force from the tackle equals the mass of the tackler multiplied by their velocity. In football, a heavier player running slow can hit as hard as a lighter player running fast.

A tackler forces a runner out of bounds by crouching down and pushing up into the runner's chest.

Torque

One of the best ways to tackle is to generate torque. Torque is the force that makes an object revolve around its axis of rotation, which is always near the object's center. A low or high tackle can produce torque. A low tackle that knocks the runner's feet backward will cause their upper body to rotate forward. They will rotate forward in the opposite direction, lifting their feet off the ground. In the same way, a hit into the chest or shoulders drives the upper body back. Torque forces the legs to swing forward, knocking the player off their feet.

Center of Mass

Low and high tackles are hard to resist. A player's center of mass is concentrated in the center of their body. A hard-enough hit on the center of mass will push a player backward. It may knock them over, but it will not be as destructive as a hit higher or lower. This is because such hits will not produce rotation. It will therefore use more energy to produce the same result. This is not good news for defenders, who have to keep making tackles throughout a 60-minute game.

GETTING PHYSICAL: LINE OF SCRIMMAGE

Players in the line of scrimmage crouch down so their center of mass is close to the ground. By crouching, they have lower potential torque than if they were standing up. This keeps the opposition from getting beneath their center of mass. It also makes it easier for them to push over a player who is standing or running. The standing player's center of mass is farther away from their axis of rotation, which makes it easier for a tackler to generate torque.

Impact!

Many NFL players weigh more than 300 pounds (136 kg). Some of the quicker players, such as defensive backs, are more likely to be about 200 pounds (91 kg). The average defensive back can run 40 yards (37 m) in 4.56 seconds. That means that even an average-sized player can generate up to 1,600 pounds (726 kg) of tackling force.

Acceleration of Impact

The acceleration of an impact is measured in units of gravity (g). On this scale, 1 g is the acceleration due to gravity on Earth's surface. Someone on a high-g roller coaster might experience up to 6.3 g. In a fighter jet, up to 10 g. In a tackle, the tackled player's head can accelerate inside his helmet at 30 to 60 g, and even up to more than 100 g. Even when players are wearing helmets, this can cause a serious risk of concussion.

Concussion

A concussion is temporary damage to the brain caused by an impact. The person may not lose consciousness, but their brain stops working as it normally would. One common symptom is confusion. Another is not being able to remember anything about the impact. Other symptoms include loss of memory, and poor judgment, balance, and speech. Most times, the damage is for a short time. It passes after the player rests. But, after a first concussion, a second concussion can cause permanent damage. A concussion is up to six times more likely to happen in a player who has already suffered one.

Officials use flashlights to check whether a player's eyes respond correctly to a beam of light. If they do not respond, this may be a sign of a concussion.

Some concussions are inevitable. Players crash into one another or fall to the ground, hitting their head.

About 34 percent of college football players have had at least one concussion. Some professional players have had so many, they show signs of brain damage. Some have even taken legal action.

The NFL now has tests to help. These tests help coaches know if a player has suffered a concussion. Guidelines say that a concussed player cannot play until they recover.

GETTING PHYSICAL: WARNING LIGHTS

Any significant blow to the head can cause a concussion. But, football is so fast that it can be difficult to keep track of collisions. Sometimes, players do not even know themselves that they have suffered a hit. Science can help. Some teams place sensors in players' helmets that detect a collision. The sensors are linked to lights in the padding at the base of the helmet. If the helmet suffers a significant impact, the lights flash. This tells officials that a player needs to leave the field, then get analyzed for concussion.

Chase with Pythagoras

If the quarterback makes the right play, they can get the ball to a receiver or running back with an open field. Now it is a straight race for the end zone between the runner and the defender. It is a sprint. Athletes accelerate to the greatest velocity they can sustain over the distance.

Catching Up

The defender is often at a great disadvantage. They can be far away by the time a running back breaks the line, or by the time they know which receiver will get the ball. They have to play catch-up. But, they have an unexpected weapon on their side: a theorem. The theorem was figured out by mathematician Pythagoras, in the sixth century B.C.E.

When a receiver gets the ball, they run straight downfield. This is the shortest line to the end zone. For a defender, the route is not as clear.

A Right-Angled Triangle

The Pythagorean theorem is a law about right-angled triangles. The two sides of the triangle that meet in a right angle are called the legs. They are usually labeled a and b. The longer side opposite the right angle is called the hypotenuse, labeled c. Pythagoras figured out that if the length of each leg is squared, or multiplied by itself, and the two squares are added together, they equal the square of the hypotenuse. The equation is written as $a^2 + b^2 = c^2$. Calculating the square root of c^2 gives the length of the hypotenuse.

How does that help a defender? Let's imagine that a receiver and a defender start running from the same line on the field, but the defender is 30 yards (27 m) away from the receiver. The line between them is the base leg of a triangle. The receiver has 40 yards (37 m) to the end zone. The receiver's route is the upright leg of the triangle. The path the defender has to take to intercept the receiver is the hypotenuse. This can be shown as (30 x 30) + (40 x 40) = 2,500. The square root of 2,500 is 50, which is the distance in yards the defender must cover. They need to run at the right speed to make sure they catch the attacker before the line.

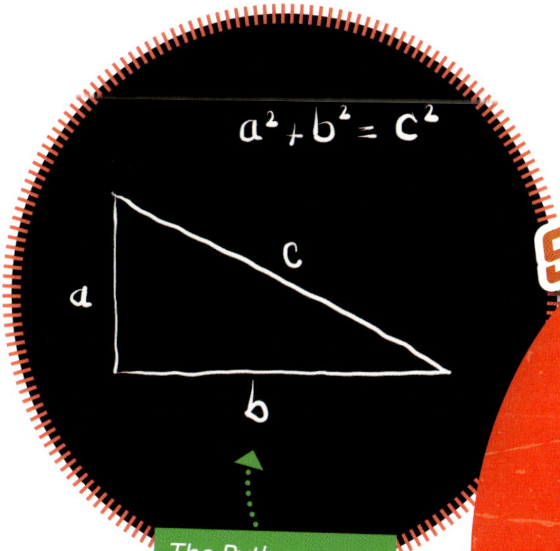

The Pythagorean theorem is still used to figure out land area.

SCIENCE WINS!

WATSON SAVES THE DAY

In 2006, Ben Watson of the New England Patriots ran nearly the length of the field to tackle Broncos cornerback Champ Bailey. Bailey had run 100 yards (91 m) on an interception. Watson followed the most efficient course that would intercept Bailey. After tracking him the whole length of the field, Watson hauled Bailey down at the 1-yard (0.9 m) line, saving the Patriots from a touchdown.

CHAPTER 6

TRACKING PERFORMANCE

Football coaches know that any tiny advantage could help them gain victory. They try to leave nothing to chance. They condition their athletes, study the opposition, and come up with dozens and dozens of plays. To do all this as effectively as possible, they rely on knowledge. That is where science comes in.

Using GPS

At school or college level, many players wear small Global Positioning System (GPS) trackers. These trackers record every move they make in training or in games. The tracker is a small device, often worn inside a compression shirt at the back of the shoulder pads. It measures a player's movement and speed by bouncing signals off satellites in orbit above Earth. This information is speed, and it goes into computers.

Coaches use headphones and microphones to pass messages to each other, and to players on the field.

Then, computer programs show coaches information, such as where a player spends their time or how often they sprint during a game.

Other programs are even more advanced. NFL teams gather **real-time data**, such as information about a player's body temperature and physical condition. Conditioning coaches can use this data to spot potential health problems in their players, and which players need more physical training.

Crunching the Numbers

Data analysts are now part of every football team. They use customized programs to give them data on athletes. They also use computer technology to study hundreds of plays, and look at their own team and at the opposition. Then, they use the information to figure out where they can improve. Technology companies know the rewards can be high. Television networks are also looking to get an edge over their rivals in sports coverage. The NFL knows that it can sell the networks in-game **statistics**, which could also attract bigger audiences. Fans love to see statistics about the game.

Coaches track the success or failure of plays. They also track the physical condition of their players.

Getting Technical

If you watch football, you may have seen coaches with tablets. Tablets allow coaches to analyze plays. They do this right after they have happened.

The Digital Era

Football is big business. In 2014, one of the biggest computer companies in the world, Microsoft, was given a contract to provide Surface Pro 2 tablets to all the teams. Each team got 25 tablets—13 for the sidelines of the field and another 12 for the coaching staff in the stands.

Special Features

The tablets are like regular tablets, but they have some differences. They do not connect to the Internet, for security reasons. They also run only one program. This program captures color images and video of the current game. The footage is sent through a secure radiofrequency identification (RFID) system to the coaches, who then use it to review plays. They can use a special "pen" to mark the screen with arrows or other symbols. Selected images can then be sent to the tablets down by the field. These images get studied by the players themselves. For example, linemen can check to see if they are lining up in the best position, or quarterbacks can look for areas where the defense is weak.

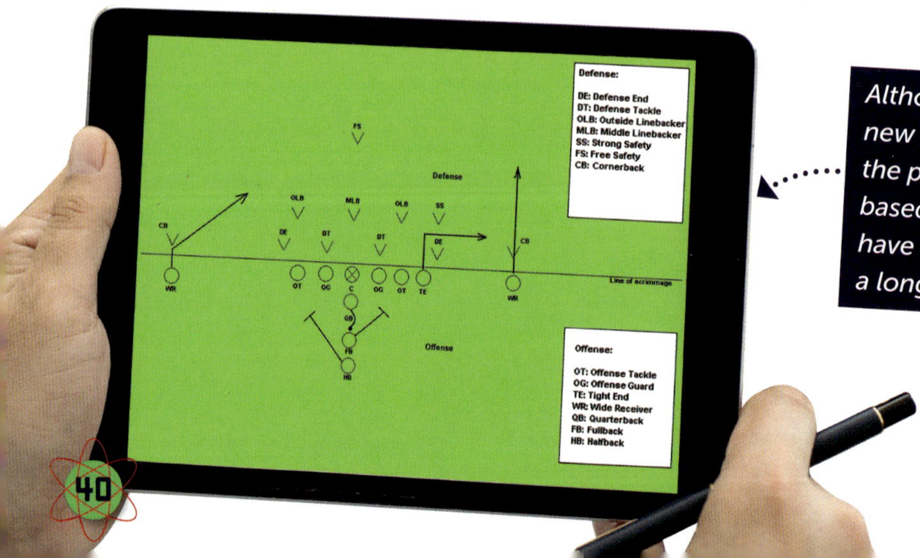

Although the NFL uses new tablet technology, the play book is usually based on moves that have been around for a long time.

During a game, coaches share printouts containing data about players.

Football-Proofed

The tablets had to be glareproof, so they could be read in sunshine or under floodlights. They also had to be rain and snowproof. The blue casing has a special handle so that players can keep hold of it even when they are wearing gloves. The casing is rubber so that, if it is dropped, it will not get badly damaged.

GETTING PHYSICAL: SENSORS

RFID sensors go in the back of players' shoulder pads. The sensors use GPS to detect all sorts of movement, as well as acceleration and impact. They also track players' real-time health. The data is transferred to receivers on the sidelines, and appears on computers for coaches. It is not only players whose movements get tracked. In 2016, an NFL trial put sensors inside the football. This made it possible to tell how fast the ball was traveling.

Virtual Reality

Anyone can practice throwing to a friend. But, a professional quarterback needs dozens of players to practice. That is not realistic because others have to do their own training. Luckily, science now has the answer.

Simulators

A general manager for the Denver Broncos remembered his training in the U.S. Air Force. Fighter pilots train in machines called **simulators**. They respond as they fly over real-time footage of landscapes. They can learn to fly without leaving the ground. Why not build a simulator for quarterbacks, too?

One day, virtual reality (VR) will allow fans to experience the thrill of being in the middle of a game.

The technology is built into a helmet, which has a special visor that gives the quarterback a realistic view of the field. The view includes other players. The technology can program the players to follow NFL plays made over the last 10 years. The quarterback watches the snap, then throws a real football to simulate the pass they would throw in the game. The ball hits a net while sensors measure its direction and speed. The system uses an **algorithm** to calculate the precise path the ball would have taken. It also determines whether it would have reached its intended receiver. The system also follows the quarterback's own movements, such as tracking what would happen if they ran out of the pocket.

A Better Player

The system has many benefits. It allows the quarterback to practice throwing different kinds of passes. The repetition helps create muscle memory. This means that the athlete's arm "learns" how hard to throw the ball. The repetition also helps their understanding of the game. Repetition can sharpen their detection of movement out of the corner of their eye. It can also improve their decision making. They can become used to how to act in different situations.

SCIENCE WINS!

BRADY'S BEST

At Super Bowl LI in 2017, the Patriots' Tom Brady had his second-most successful game ever. He completed 28 passes of 48 attempts and threw a Super Bowl record of 505 yards (462 m) in total. Brady's old coach says that the quarterback is not a natural athlete. He says that Brady practices hard and works to understand the game. He is also able to take in a lot of information about what is happening in front of him. This is thanks to spending thousands of hours training, including the use of VR. But, in this case, it did not help. The Patriots still lost to the Philadelphia Eagles.

GET PHYSICAL!

It is time to find out for yourself something about the science of football. In this experiment, you will learn about how a football bounces and why it is so difficult to recover a fumble. You can do this experiment by yourself, but it might be more fun to try it with a friend or a group of friends.

YOU WILL NEED:

- Small mints that are oval in shape, like Tic Tacs®
- A smooth table
- A video camera or phone camera

Instructions

1. Set up the camera or phone so that it can record the tabletop, or ask a friend to hold it.

2. Hold a mint about 2 feet (0.6 m) above the table.

3. As you drop the mint, record a video of how it bounces until it comes to a standstill.

4. Repeat the experiment with another mint.

5. Watch the bouncing mint on the video. It might help to watch on a large screen. For each bounce, guess whether it was higher or lower than the one before it.

6. If you have a football, you can repeat the same experiment by dropping the football on a flat, even patch of ground and recording a video of the results.

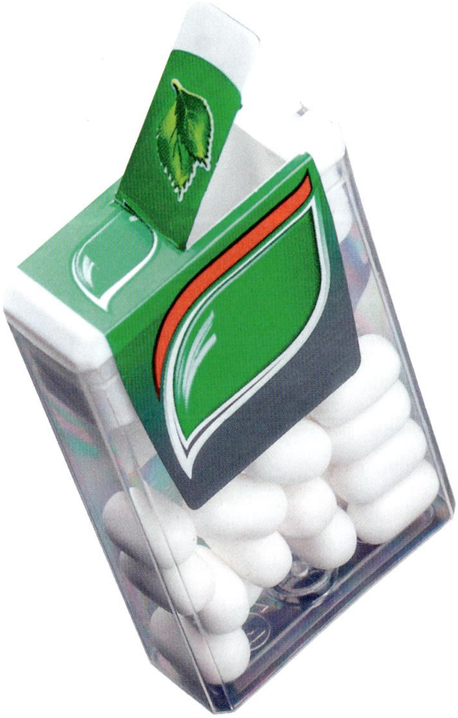

Analysis

Did the mint bounce highest on its first bounce? Why might it bounce to different heights each time?

Conclusion

You probably noticed that the mint bounced higher on some bounces than on others. This is unusual. If an object were completely round, it would bounce a little lower on each bounce. But, when an object is more oblong-shaped, like the mint or a football, the bounce is less even. Even a small change in the angle at which the mint hits the table can start it spinning. If the mint starts spinning, that uses up some of its energy. That means there is less energy to raise it back into the air. If the next bounce keeps the mint from spinning, its energy goes into the bounce, which will likely be higher.

Whether you are playing with your friends in the park or on the field in an NFL stadium, the ball still bounces in an unpredictable way.

When you hold the mint, it has a fixed amount of potential energy, which is energy it has as a result of its height and the possibility it will fall. When you drop the mint, the potential energy becomes kinetic energy. If the mint is spinning, some of its kinetic energy goes into making it spin. Only the leftover energy goes into making it bounce.

GLOSSARY

acceleration The rate of change in the velocity of an object by speeding up, slowing down, or changing direction while in motion

air resistance A force that acts in the opposite direction of an object traveling through the air, slowing it down

algorithm A set of step-by-step rules

arc Part of a smooth curve

axis An imaginary line around which an object rotates

bladders Organs in the body where urine is stored. In sports, they are the inflated, hollow bag inside a ball.

center of mass The point in the middle of an object's mass

cleats Small projections on the bottom of a shoe

data Information

down One of the four chances that a football team has to move forward when it is their turn to have the ball

force An interaction that changes the motion of something

friction The resistance of one object moving over another

fulcrum The point against which a lever is placed to turn

gravity A force that attracts things toward the center of Earth, or toward any other physical body

Hail Mary A long pass thrown in a desperate attempt to score

impact The action of one object coming into contact with another object

impulse An amount of force applied to an object over a length of time

inertia The quality of a moving body that makes it stay in motion, or in a stationary body that makes it stay still

kinematics The study of the motion of objects

kinetic energy The energy an object has because of its motion

lever A rigid bar resting on a pivot or fulcrum used to move a load

ligaments The tissues that connect bones

line of scrimmage An imaginary line across the field that players cannot cross until the next play has begun

mass The quantity of matter in an object (its "weight")

midriff The front of a person's body between the chest and the waist

molecules Particles formed by atoms bonding together

momentum The quantity of motion of a body, measured as a product of its mass and velocity

offensive drive The series of plays that a team does when they have the football in their possession

parabola The curved path made by an object thrown through the air

physics The branch of science that studies materials and energy

pocket The place where the quarterback stands, just behind the center, after receiving the ball

real-time The actual time during which something takes place

rosin A sticky substance

simulators Machines that provide realistic imitations of operating a vehicle or an aircraft

snap The backward passing of the football at the start of play

spiral A continuous curve around a central axis

statistics The science of collecting and analyzing data in the form of numbers

streamlined Designed to pass smoothly though air or water

studs Small projections attached to the bottom of sports shoes

synthetic Artificial

torque The force that causes objects to rotate around an axis

velocity The speed of something in a specific direction

vestibular system Structures in the inner ear that help with balance

LEARNING MORE

Find out more about the physics of football.

Books

Martin, Brett S. *STEM in Football* (STEM in Sports). ABDO Publishing, 2017.

McClafferty, Carla Killough. *Fourth Down and Inches: Concussions and Football's Make-or-Break Moment*. Carolrhoda Books, 2013.

McCollum, Sean. *Full STEAM Football: Science, Technology, Engineering, Arts, and Mathematics of the Game* (Full STEAM Sports). Capstone Press, 2018.

Stuckey, Rachel. *Be a Force on the Field: Skills, Drills, and Plays*. Crabtree Publishing, 2016.

Websites

Watch videos about science in football, including catching, at:
www.chevronstemzone.com/football

Read a guide to the physics in play during any football game at:
https://entertainment.howstuffworks.com/physics-of-football.htm

Read a scientist's explanation about throwing the perfect pass at:
www.sciencebuddies.org/blog/the-science-of-football-flight

INDEX